Valley of
the Kings

digging
for the past

BRIAN FAGAN
General Editor

Valley of the Kings

Stuart Tyson Smith
and Nancy Stone Bernard

OXFORD
UNIVERSITY PRESS

To Spencer
and to Sarah and Deneen

OXFORD
UNIVERSITY PRESS

Oxford   New York
Auckland   Bangkok   Buenos Aires   Cape Town   Chennai
Dar es Salaam   Delhi   Hong Kong   Istanbul   Karachi   Kolkata
Kuala Lumpur   Madrid   Melbourne   Mexico City   Mumbai   Nairobi
São Paulo   Shanghai   Singapore   Taipei   Tokyo   Toronto

Copyright © 2003 by Oxford University Press
Published by Oxford University Press, Inc.
198 Madison Avenue, New York, New York   10016
www.oup.com

Oxford is a registered trademark of Oxford University Press

Design: Kingsley Parker
Layout: Lenny Levitsky
Picture research: Jennifer Smith

Library of Congress Cataloging-in-Publication Data

Smith, Stuart Tyson
Valley of the Kings / Stuart Tyson Smith and Nancy Stone Bernard.
p. cm. — (Digging for the past)
Summary: Explores Egypt's Valley of the Kings, a vast burial ground
containing more than seventy tombs, and discusses archaeologists'
findings and challenges during nearly two hundred years of excavation.
Includes bibliographical references and index.
ISBN 0-19-514770-7 (alk. paper)
1. Valley of the Kings (Egypt)--Juvenile literature. [1. Valley of the
Kings (Egypt) 2. Egypt--Antiquities. 3. Archaeology.] I. Bernard, Nancy
S. (Nancy Stone) II. Title. III. Series.   3. Excavations (Archaeology)
DT73.B44 S66 2002
932'-dc21
255   2002004288
9 8 7 6 5 4 3 2 1
Printed in Hong Kong on acid-free paper

Cover: Against the back-drop of Valley of the Kings, Howard Carter and his assistant examine the nested coffins of Tutankhamun.
Frontispiece: A view of the Tutankhamun cache site in 1907.

Picture Credits: Giraudon/Art Resource, NY: 11, 13; Erich Lessing/Art Resource, NY: cover, 20, 39; Scala/Art Resource, NY: 3, 14, 17, 18, 19, 22, 46; Courtesy of Nancy Stone Bernard: 40 bottom; Birmingham City Archives, Benjamin Stone Collection: 16; © Boltin Picture Library: 8, 27b, 28; Frank Spooner Agency: 43; Griffith Institute, Oxford: cover inset, 24, 25, 26; Heritage Images/©The British Library: 4, 5, 12; Heritage Images/© The British Museum: 9, 10, 21; The Metropolitan Museum of Art, Photography by the Egyptian Expedition: 2, 3, 27top; The Metropolitan Museum of Art: 23; New York Public Library: 15; Courtesy of Stuart Tyson Smith: 15, 29, 30, 35, 36, 40 top, 44; ©Time Pix: 34; Gary Tong: 6, 33.

 Contents

Where and When

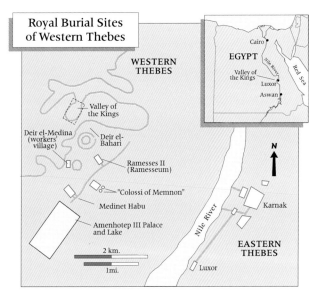

Royal Burial Sites of Western Thebes

WESTERN THEBES

EGYPT
Cairo
Nile River
Valley of the Kings
Luxor
Aswan
Red Sea

Valley of the Kings

Deir el-Medina (workers' village)

Deir el-Bahari

Ramesses II (Ramesseum)

"Colossi of Memnon"

Medinet Habu

Amenhotep III Palace and Lake

Karnak

Nile River

EASTERN THEBES

Luxor

2 km.
1mi.

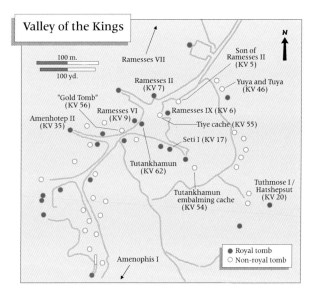

Valley of the Kings

N

100 m.
100 yd.

Ramesses VII

Son of Ramesses II (KV 5)

Ramesses II (KV 7)

Yuya and Tuya (KV 46)

"Gold Tomb" (KV 56)

Ramesses VI (KV 9)

Ramesses IX (KV 6)

Amenhotep II (KV 35)

Tiye cache (KV 55)

Seti I (KV 17)

Tutankhamun (KV 62)

Tutankhamun embalming cache (KV 54)

Tuthmose I / Hatshepsut (KV 20)

Amenophis I

● Royal tomb
○ Non-royal tomb

Archaeological History

1798 ▶
Napoleon arrives in Egypt with 4,000 soldiers and 139 scientists and artists

1824 ▶
Jean-François Champollion deciphers hieroglyphs from paper rubbings of Rosetta Stone

1881 ▶
Emile Brugsch finds more than 50 royal mummies with some 6,000 objects hidden in a tomb

1914 ▶
Gaston Maspero draws up a contract giving Lord Carnarvon and Howard Carter the right to excavate in the Valley for 10 years

1989 ▶
Kent Weeks and his team begin search for KV 5, abandoned in 1825 by an explorer who thought it unimportant

◀ **1815–1821**
Giovanni Belzoni crudely excavates Egyptian monuments and opens an Egyptian exhibit in London, which helps popularize ancient Egypt

◀ **1827**
John Gardner Wilkinson paints large numbers above entrance of every known tomb, giving the KV designations still used today

◀ **1905**
Under patron Theodore Davis, Arthur Weigall excavates tomb of Yuya and his wife Tuya, two of the best-preserved mummies found

◀ **1922**
For patron Carnarvon, Carter discovers Tutankhamun's tomb

◀ **1997**
Weeks and his team find more KV 5 corridors and estimate at least 150 rooms, more than any other tomb in Egypt

Ancient History

**Dynasty 18
(1550–1325 BC)**

1524–1518 BC
◀ Tuthmosis I's short reign is marked by military successes that set the tone for Dynasty 18

1498–1483 BC
◀ Queen Hatshepsut rules for 20 years. Her mortuary temple at Deir el-Bahari is considered the most elegant of all Egyptian monuments

1504–1450 BC
◀ Tuthmosis III shatters Hatshepsut's temples and statues, and even her name disappears from the records; he extends empire further than any king up to this time

1386–1349 BC
◀ Amenhotep III's 37-year reign is one of the most prosperous; his chief wife, Tiy, is unusually conspicuous on monuments

1350–1334 BC
◀ Akhenaten, a revolutionary, moves the capital from Thebes 300 miles north to Akhetaten (modern Tel el-Amarna) and forbids the worship of old gods

1334–1325 BC
◀ Tutankhamun—King Tut—returns the court to Thebes; little is known about him before his lavishly furnished tomb is found in 1922

**Dynasties 19 and 20
(1296–1069 BC)**

1291–1278 BC
◀ Seti I begins to regain territory in the Near East; starts the great Hypostyle Hall at Karnak; constructs his tomb, the Valley's longest and deepest

1279–1212 BC
◀ Ramesses II rules 67 years and is ancient Egypt's greatest builder, with projects at Karnak and Abu Simbel; KV 5 is built for his numerous sons

1212–1202 BC
◀ Merneptah's military campaigns are recorded at Karnak, in the Delta, and on a significant Victory stela

1182–1151 BC
◀ Ramesses III's 31-year reign in Dynasty 20 marks the end of ancient Egypt's greatness

Introduction

"**E**verywhere the glint of gold . . . wonderful things" —so thought Egyptologist Howard Carter as he looked through a tiny hole into Tutankhamun's as yet unexcavated tomb in 1922. In the early days excavators in Egypt would dig up the "wonderful things" and send them to museums and collectors in Europe and America. But today archaeologists, wherever they dig, look for clues to how people lived in ancient times, and are careful to leave the "wonderful things" in the country where they found them. They learn about the past not only from objects, called artifacts, but also from the architecture of ancient buildings, the paintings on the walls of temples and tombs, and the inscriptions on stone and papyrus.

Valley of the Kings has been called the world's most magnificent burial ground. During the period of the New Kingdom, from about 1550 to 1070 BC, in a ravine nestled under a line of dramatic cliffs directly to the west of the New Kingdom's capital, Thebes, an army of Egyptian workers dug tombs for their rulers and a few nobles. The tombs were not just caverns in the rock but had stairways, corridors, and enormous rooms, carefully dug out and decorated with carved reliefs and scenes depicting Egyptian religion. Now, some 3,000 years since Valley of the Kings was abandoned, modern Egyptologists have begun to understand how these tombs reflect the society of the ancient Egyptians, as new tombs and treasures continue to be discovered.

In 1922 Howard Carter found the stunning gold mask of Tutankhamun, the boy-king. The mask had remained untouched since the day Tut was buried more than 3,200 years earlier.

1

Tourists and Plunderers

I t is hard to imagine how people traveled the ancient world without cars, trains, or jet planes. Yet thousands of Greek and Roman tourists visited Egypt from the end of the third century BC through the second century AD. We know this from more than 2,000 Greek and Latin inscriptions, or graffiti, that these visitors left.

Many of the artifacts that Giovanni Belzoni removed from Egypt are still on display in the British Museum's sculpture gallery. In this picture from about 1820, the giant head of an Egyptian statue was just one of the many fascinating objects that awaited visitors to the museum.

After Egypt was incorporated into the Roman Empire in 30 BC, some Romans settled there. Although the Egyptian religion continued, this woman's portrait, which was set into the outermost wrappings over the head of her mummy, shows how Roman clothing, hairstyles, and jewelry had become part of Egyptian daily life.

Herodotus, a Greek often called the first historian, visited Egypt in the fifth century BC. Egyptian writings called hieroglyphs were still in use and like later tourists, Herodotus hired a guide and interpreter to translate what he observed. His mass of information and misinformation was written around 460–455 BC.

In AD 130 Roman Emperor Hadrian visited Egypt carrying a guidebook by the Roman author Diodorus Siculus. Diodorus's contemporary, the geographer Strabo, also wrote about his visit to Valley of the Kings. But none of these tourists knew that, as early as 1100 BC, professional thieves had opened most of the royal tombs in the Valley and looted their contents so thoroughly that most royal treasures were lost forever.

By the time the Roman Empire became Christian, hieroglyphs were no longer used, and soon their meaning was lost. By the late fourth century AD, people regarded the ancient Egyptian religion as sinful, and they ruthlessly obliterated monument inscriptions, as well as sculpted faces, heads, hands, and feet with hammer and chisel. It was almost 1,000 years before explorers realized that Valley of the Kings was an important part of an ancient civilization.

In 1798 the French general Napoleon arrived in Egypt with a 4,000-man army and a team of 139 scientists and artists, in an undertaking called the French Expedition. Napoleon was at war with the English and realized that one of the ways to win the war was to control Egypt. By August 1799, Napoleon was forced to retreat from Egypt after the English admiral Lord Nelson destroyed the French fleet at the Battle of the Nile.

Although the French army had left Egypt, the scholars and artists of the French Expedition had collected enough information to publish, between 1809 and 1813, 24 volumes titled *Description de l'Egypte* (Description of Egypt), which introduced the world to Egyptian antiquities. The other important result of Napoleon's invasion was a French officer's discovery of the Rosetta Stone. This engraved stone later led to the decipherment of the mysterious hieroglyphs that appeared on the monuments.

After the French-British conflict ended, tourists and entrepreneurs arrived: collectors, merchants, and some dishonest dealers who saw that a profit could be made from the antiquities trade. The dealers stripped thousands of portable stones and statues, reliefs, and obelisks, as well as papyri, and sold them to museums and private collectors in Europe and the Americas.

Giovanni Belzoni was one of those entrepreneurs. Six foot six and clever, Belzoni got his first job as a circus strongman. He arrived in Egypt in 1815 and, when his scheme to interest the Egyptians in a waterwheel failed, he turned to archaeology. In the next four years he made some of the most exciting discoveries

In this 1799 painting, some French soldiers take a break near an Egyptian ruin. When the advancing French soldiers first saw the impressive temples of Luxor and Karnak at Thebes, across the Nile from Valley of the Kings, they burst into applause.

Despite his strongman reputation and slipshod methods, Belzoni precisely copied this drawing from the walls of the tomb of Seti I in the Valley.

world had ever seen. Unlike many of his contemporaries, he attempted to document his finds, and his illustrated book showed a genuine interest in ancient Egypt.

Belzoni discovered eight tombs in Valley of the Kings, including those of Ramesses I and of Seti I, the father of Ramesses II, known as Ramesses the Great. The Seti I tomb proved to be the finest yet found in the Valley. Its architecture was perfectly proportioned, the floors were littered with the king's funerary equipment, and the walls were brightly painted. At its center was the king's shining alabaster sarcophagus, nine feet long and three feet wide, beautifully decorated with text that could not be read at that time. Soon after, a flash flood washed through the tomb. But in spite of the flood and damage by early explorers, it is still one of the most spectacular tombs in the Valley. Today, however, because of the buildup of groundwater, its walls and roof are unstable.

Despite his terrible methods—which resulted in the destruction of numerous monuments and artifacts—Belzoni sent an enormous number of Egyptian antiquities back to London. In 1821 he opened his Egyptian exhibit in Piccadilly (one of London's most crowded thoroughfares), which helped popularize ancient Egypt. But the exhibit was not as successful as Belzoni had hoped. The huge sculptures were auctioned to individuals and institutions. Many of Belzoni's small finds can be seen today in the British Museum's impressive sculpture gallery.

This wall painting from the tomb of Seti I depicts the beaked god Thoth (left), who oversaw the judgment of the dead, greeting the Pharaoh. This scene survived in all its glory, but some of the paintings in Seti I's tomb were damaged from "squeezes"—impressions made of the relief carving using wet paper—taken by Belzoni and later visitors.

2

Explorers, Observers, and Patrons

In this 19th-century painting, Champollion (reclining in the foreground) and his 1828–29 French-Italian expedition document and read inscriptions on the monuments around them.

I n contrast to Belzoni, John Gardner Wilkinson, considered one of the fathers of modern Egyptology, was not interested in the plundering and removal of antiquities. Instead, he began the careful scientific recording of the monuments. In 1824, when Wilkinson came to Egypt, the decipherment of hieroglyphs, initiated by the brilliant Frenchman Jean-François Champollion was making it possible to see the monuments as more than architecture. Once the hieroglyphs could be read, they explained some of the history and thinking of the ancient people.

Wilkinson was an amateur scholar but one with a great interest in Egyptian antiquities. In 1827, with a brush and a bucket of red paint, he walked through the Valley writing large numbers above the entrance of every tomb he could find. Wilkinson painted KV and a number on 21 tombs and 7 more entrances. The KV stands for Kings' Valley, and it is the system still used today. The most recent number, KV 62, was given to the tomb of Tutankhamun.

In 1829, Champollion and his French-Italian expedition arrived in Egypt and Valley of the Kings. At last, Champollion could read on the tombs and monuments the hieroglyphs that up to then he had seen only on paper copies. He made his headquarters in the tomb of Ramesses VI for two months, copying scenes and their details.

Belzoni and Champollion thought that they had found all the tombs in the Valley. Ironically, it was the Ramesses VI tomb where Champollion made his headquarters that hid the most spectacular tomb ever found. The concealed tomb of King Tut was only a few feet below where he camped.

In 1835 the Egyptian government passed an ordinance to protect government-owned artifacts and put a stop to the plundering of archaeological sites. The Egyptian Antiquities Service was established in 1855. In 1899, Gaston Maspero, director of the Service, appointed the young archaeologist Howard Carter as Chief Inspector of Antiquities of Upper Egypt. Carter was

A manuscript page from the French decipherer Champollion's Grammaire égyptienne *(Egyptian grammar) shows some of the figures that enabled him to read hieroglyphs.*

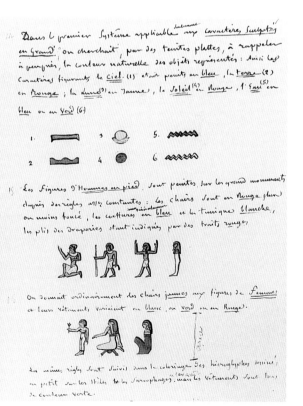

responsible for overseeing digs in the upper Nile Valley. Carter thought that one of the duties of an Egyptologist should be conservation: tombs should not only be protected and restored but also lit by electric light so that tourists could view them properly. One of Carter's achievements was the introduction of lighting into the six best tombs in the Valley.

This was an era during which archaeologists had to find wealthy patrons to finance their digs, as funds from the Egyptian Antiquities Service were negligible. One of the key patrons was Theodore R. Davis, a wealthy 65-year-old American lawyer. From 1902 to 1914 Davis found willing experts to dig for him, and together they made

Despite Egypt's hot climate, early-20th-century excavators dressed in suits and ties. From right to left, Edward Russell Ayrton, Davis's excavator; wealthy patron Theodore Davis; and Arthur Weigall and his wife, Hortense, stand in front of the entrance to the tomb of Ramesses IV.

some important discoveries. His first excavator was Howard Carter.

In 1902, under Davis's sponsorship, Carter found a tomb with the remains of two Dynasty 22 mummies contained in a double coffin. Although it was not an important find, Davis was hooked. In 1903, the last work that Carter undertook for Davis was to explore KV 20. The dig was expensive and time-consuming, but the results were extraordinary. The tomb extends 630 feet into the rock, and it is one of the longest and largest tombs in Egypt. Now we know that it was initially prepared for Tuthmosis I, father of Queen Hatshepsut, and later enlarged for the queen herself.

Soon after, the Antiquities Service transferred Carter to northern Egypt. Davis replaced him with the well-trained James Edward Quibell. However, Quibell, probably the most qualified archaeologist to work in the Valley at the beginning of the 20th century, did not like working for a treasure-hunter like Davis, and soon transferred to another part of Egypt. He was replaced by Arthur Weigall, an assistant to the outstanding archaeologist Flinders Petrie.

In a promising area, Weigall directed about 60 workmen to cut into a mound of chippings. After 17 days, they exposed the top of a sealed door. Most of the workmen had gone home for the day when Weigall and the foreman broke through its seal. The opening was so small that only the foreman's young son could climb through it. After removing his turban (which most Upper Egyptians wore at that time and still do), he was small enough to be lowered through the hole on a sash placed under his arms. At first he cried, but became quiet when he saw golden artifacts as he reached the tomb floor.

Many statues of Queen Hatshepsut, including this one, were broken and defaced by her successor. Davis and Carter explored her enormous tomb, KV 20, in 1903.

Sumptuously gilded and decorated with glass and stone inlays, Tuya's mask was in perfect condition after 3,300 years.

The men shouted down to him to pick up what he could. He did, and when he was pulled back up he was holding treasures, including a gold-covered chariot yoke and a magnificently crafted staff. (Today's archaeologists shudder at the idea of sending someone into a tomb to pick up artifacts this way, as it is very important to record exactly where each object is found.) Weigall and others stood guard that night, worried that robbers would invade the tomb.

The next day the workmen opened the doorway and cleared the stairwell. Carrying candles, Gaston Maspero, head of the Egyptian Antiquities Service, and Davis stepped into the chamber, where they found inscriptions showing that this was the tomb of Yuya and his wife Tuya, parents of Queen Tiy, beloved wife of Amenhotep III and mother of the philosopher pharaoh, Akhenaten.

Robbers had opened their wooden coffins in antiquity. But the thieves had been more interested in jewelry on the mummies, which lay inside the coffins, than in the mummies themselves. Davis, Maspero, and Weigall looked down at the amazingly well-preserved, lifelike mummies of Yuya and Tuya. Peering around, they saw that the tiny chamber was stacked to the ceiling with funerary equipment decorated with sparkling gold and silver.

Artifacts were beautifully preserved—even honey in a pot smelled fresh. They spotted a chair of richly polished red wood decorated with gilded figures of musicians and, on its back, the figure of a princess. Reading the hieroglyphs, they realized that the chair had belonged to the sister of Tutankhamun, who had it put in

Workers in the Afterlife

The Egyptian name for mummy-shaped funerary figurines, *ushabti* or *shawabti*, means answerer, indicating that they would magically answer when called to perform work for the deceased. The Egyptians believed that the gods required the dead to work, tilling and harvesting the celestial fields. But who wants to work away their afterlife? Egyptians just wanted to have fun after they were dead. So some enterprising grave-goods salesman came up with the idea of ushabtis.

Ushabtis were most commonly made of wood, stone, and faience, a ceramic material often glazed bright blue. A special spell from the Egyptian *Book of the Dead*, which contained crucial information needed for success in the afterlife, activated these magical figurines. If the gods called upon the deceased to till the celestial fields, dig a canal, or harvest the crops, they would just say the spell and the ushabti would jump to life, say, "Here I am, here I am!" and go right to work.

Grave-goods suppliers even provided special tools for ushtabis—miniature hoes and yokes with baskets. Just to make sure, the salesmen started recommending that their clients get more than one ushabti: after all, what if one got tired? Eventually there were 365, one for each day of the year. But what if the right ushabti did not show up on the right day? And what if some lazy ushabtis did not show up at all? That was not a problem: an extra fee would buy one overseer for every 10 workers, for a total of 401.

Princess Sitamun donated this beautifully carved chair for the burial of her grandparents. Yuya and Tuya's royal connections made theirs one of the richest tombs in Egypt.

the tomb of her grandparents. Davis was credited with finding the finest burial ever.

Quibell returned to the Valley to help clear the tomb. One day in 1905 a simply dressed old woman visited the tomb accompanied by a Frenchman who addressed her as "Your Highness." The archaeologist apologized that there was nothing for them to sit on. The elderly woman spotted the Princess chair and said that would be fine and sat down. Fortunately, the ancient stringed seat held up. Quibell was too embarrassed to tell his visitor not to sit on this 3,000-year-old chair. Later he learned that the "old woman" was Empress Eugénie of France, wife of Napoléon III and the guest of honor at an upcoming Suez Canal ceremony. Thus another queen was the last person to sit upon that ancient chair before it and the rest of the contents of the tomb of Yuya and Tuya were removed to the Cairo Museum.

Davis's archaeologists continued to make amazing finds. Next, he employed a well-trained young English archaeologist, Edward Russell Ayrton. In 1907 Davis's team discovered a single chamber, KV 55. Within was a large dismantled shrine of gilded wood that Akhenaten had prepared for his mother, Queen Tiy. There was also a collapsed inlaid royal coffin from which all identifying cartouches (oval loops in which royal names were inscribed in hieroglyphs) had been removed; only tiny pieces were left. This was a very complicated archaeological situation, but Davis, always in a hurry, did not understand the importance of careful documentation and conservation. Because of his carelessness, even today experts disagree about who was the occupant of KV 55.

In 1907 Ayrton and Davis also found a small abandoned pit, dubbed KV 54. Inside, there were about a dozen large storage jars containing small clay seals impressed with the cartouche of Tutankhamun. There were also 50 sacks of natron (the salt used for embalming), linen bandages, offering cups, bones from joints of meat (probably consumed at the funeral feast), and faded floral collars. Davis felt that the pit must have been used by thieves to hide materials from the Tutankhamun tomb after it was robbed. Davis was convinced that this was all that was left of the tomb of Tutankhamun.

Priests placed food, such as this basket of figs and dates, in tombs to reinforce the belief that the deceased would never go hungry in the afterlife.

Soon after this discovery, Davis gave a dinner party at his elegant headquarters in the Valley. Davis casually held up the 3,000-year-old floral collars from what he thought was Tutankhamun's tomb. He pulled at them to show his guests how strong they were. Of course, they disintegrated. Fortunately, three of them survived and are now at the Metropolitan Museum in New York City.

The "Gold Tomb" was another of Davis's startling discoveries. In 1908 excavator Ayrton found KV 56, another single-chamber tomb, from which he recovered the most spectacular group of Dynasty 19 jewelry ever found. The "Gold Tomb" was the pinnacle of Davis's Egyptian career.

Davis was convinced that the Valley was "exhausted." Ironically, his last excavator stopped work within six feet of what would be the sensation of the century. Davis died in 1914. Just eight years later, Howard Carter discovered Tutankhamun's tomb.

3

Sensation of the Century

This painting in Tutankhamun's burial chamber shows Ay (far right), who became the next pharaoh, performing the "Opening of the Mouth Ceremony" on the deceased King Tut.

George Herbert was the only son of Henry Herbert, the fourth Earl of Carnarvon, and his wife Evelyn. In 1890, at the age of 24, the young man succeeded to his title and inherited an immense fortune. He married Almina Wombell and they had a daughter, Evelyn. When he was 35, he was severely injured in an auto-racing accident from which he never fully recovered. He spent the rest of his life as a semi-invalid. In 1903 he visited Egypt for health reasons and soon was dabbling in Egyptology.

Carnarvon realized he was an amateur and needed the help and advice of someone knowledgeable and experienced. By 1906, Howard Carter had resigned from the Egyptian Antiquities Service. He lived in Luxor, and painted watercolors and made drawings of monuments for friends and patrons. He also kept an expert eye on the antiquities trade. Gaston Maspero, the chief of the Egyptian Antiquities Service, introduced Carter to the wealthy Earl of Carnarvon. Soon Lord Carnarvon was building a collection that eventually became one of the century's finest.

In 1914, Gaston Maspero resigned from the Antiquities Service. Before he left, he drew up a contract between the Service and Lord Carnarvon that allowed Carnarvon, under Carter's daily direction, the right to excavate for 10 years in Valley of the Kings. Soon after, Carter and Carnarvon planned an expensive first season in the Valley, employing some 300 men to remove huge dumps of chippings that other excavators had piled up over unexcavated portions of the Valley. Carter and Carnarvon were looking for the few tombs that had not been discovered, including that of Tutankhamun.

In 1914, World War I interrupted archaeological activity in Egypt and many promising archaeologists were killed during the four-year conflict. In December 1917, Lord Carnarvon's excavations in the Valley resumed. It took a month for a large gang of workmen to clear away the debris from Carter's carefully chosen location. They used a prefabricated railway. Teams of men pushed trucks along the rails and took hundreds of carloads down the Valley.

Not until 1920 did Carter once again employ large gangs to clear more rubble. Carnarvon arrived in Thebes just as Carter found a cache of 13 alabaster vases of Ramesses II and his son Merneptah. These elegant vessels were probably the most beautiful things that Carter had yet found

A talented artist, the young Howard Carter got his first job working for the Egypt Exploration Fund at Deir el-Bahari, where he painted this figure of Queen Hatshepsut's grandmother.

for Carnarvon. Lady Evelyn, Lord Carnarvon's wife, was so excited by the find that she insisted on personally digging out the artifacts. But few moments were as dramatic as this. Carter's team continued to excavate in various places in the Valley, but with no major results to show his patron.

In the summer of 1922 Carter returned to England to visit Carnarvon. He found that his patron had lost his zest for the project. He had received very little for his huge outlay of funds. But Carter thought it worthwhile to investigate the village of workmen's huts that had flourished during Dynasty 19. It was not just a last-ditch effort to find treasure. Carter, the meticulous planner, wanted to complete this long-term job. Now 48, he hoped to retire and write a huge volume about the valley he knew so well. Carter persuaded Carnarvon to invest for "one more season." The earl was a weary invalid of 56, so in the fall Carter returned to Egypt on his own.

Lord Carnarvon, here resting his legs, and Howard Carter shared an interest in Egyptology, but the men were quite different. Carnarvon, who was educated at Eton and Cambridge, lived in one of the finest homes in England. Carter had little formal education and came from a rural family of painters who specialized in animal portraits.

Carter put his men to work near the tomb of Ramesses VI, clearing away the debris from the trench where they had worked the year before. After several days of digging, they reached the level of ancient workmen's huts and the undisturbed rock and sand that lay underneath. Soon they found steps to a tomb, although Carter could not be sure it was a finished one.

At the bottom of the steps the men found a sealed doorway. Carter made a small hole at the top of the doorway and shone a flashlight into the opening. He could see far into the passageway that ran right under the tomb of Ramesses VI. It was filled with debris, an indication that it had not been disturbed since ancient times. He immediately reburied the doorway, thus missing the Tutankhamun cartouches at the bottom of the door. Alone in the moonlight, he rode his horse back to his house and pondered whether this tomb was something special.

Carter realizes, as he peers into the gilded shrines surrounding Tut's sarcophagus, that no one has entered this tomb belonging to Tutankhamun for thousands of years.

Despite his doubts, he took a chance. The next day Carter sent a telegram to Carnarvon: "At last have made a wonderful discovery in Valley; a magnificent tomb with seals intact . . . congratulations." It would take weeks for Carnarvon to arrive, and while Carter waited he had the tomb well guarded to guarantee that no present-day robbers could enter.

Almost three weeks later, on November 23, Carnarvon arrived. Carter had uncovered the doorway for Carnarvon's personal inspection, and in doing so had found the cartouche of Tutankhamun. There was evidence that the

The gilded shrines of King Tut had been sealed since his burial. Behind this original seal were a solid gold coffin and his mummy, covered by a gold mask.

tomb had been broken into twice in antiquity. But both robber holes had been sealed, and Carter was certain that the tomb had been undisturbed since huts for storage and sleeping had been built over it, probably in early Dynasty 20, around 1141 BC, some 3,200 years earlier.

The entry held only a few items of interest, and Rex Engelback, the successor to Weigall as chief inspector, was so unimpressed that he went somewhere else on a tour of inspection. In the meantime, Carter drew and photographed the first doorway with its seal impressions and then had it taken down.

On the other side of the doorway, the descending passage was filled to the ceiling with debris. It took two days to clear the 28-foot-long hallway. Broken antiquities came to light during the clearing, including a fine Amarna-style painted wooden head of a young king, coming out of a half-open lotus flower. Later in the day they found a second sealed door, almost a replica of the first. They were standing at the entrance to the inner tomb.

Carnarvon stood just behind Carter, as did Lady Evelyn, Carnarvon's daughter. Carter made a small hole in the stone wall and tested the air for purity with the flame of his candle. He peered into the tomb as a rush of hot, ancient air came out of the darkness and made the candle flame flicker. As he struggled to focus his eyes, he realized he was seeing the glitter of treasure a few feet away. Impatiently, Carnarvon asked Carter if he could see anything. And Carter replied with what have become the most famous three words in archaeology: "Yes. Wonderful things."

Later, Carter recalled his first view of the incredibly rich tomb: "As my eyes grew accustomed to the light, details of the room within emerged slowly from the mist, strange animals, statues, and gold—everywhere the glint of gold." Among the magnificent finds were a pair of large, impressive wooden guardian statues in the image of the king painted with black resin and highlighted in gold leaf. In addition, there were musical instruments, jewelry, wine jars, writing equipment, swords, daggers, and game boards.

Four sealed funerary shrines concealed an exquisite sarcophagus, three nested coffins, the innermost of solid gold, and the masked mummy of the boy-king,

The antechamber of Tutankhamun's tomb was the first room that Carter entered. This photograph shows the room as it looked when Carter first saw its jumbled mass of artifacts, including animal-shaped couches.

Several sets of the game senet, including this ornate board, were found in Tut's tomb. The young ruler must have been an avid player.

untouched since the day of his burial. It is not surprising that the tomb was never completely robbed in ancient times, as it had been buried by chippings and workers' huts from a later period. When it was covered, it was during an era (about 1141 BC) when security in the Valley was still good.

Lord Carnarvon had made the long and strenuous trip to Egypt for the opening of the tomb but did not survive long after. In April of the following year, he was bitten by a mosquito and the bite became infected while he was shaving; blood poisoning set in. Lord Carnarvon had been in ill health for some 20 years, so when he died, it was sad but not a great surprise. Newspapers, however, eager to keep up interest in the Tutankhamun discovery, invented a tall tale. The myth was that anyone connected with the tomb—even slightly—became a victim of the tomb's "curse." The "Curse of Tutankhhamun" headlines pushed newspaper sales to new heights in the 1920s. The curse was declared "Bunkum!" by a renowned Egyptologist at the time.

When the American archaeologist James Breasted and several of his colleagues visited the tomb a few days after it was opened, they were moved to tears. What touched them was that in this one tomb were objects that reflected the luxurious court of a youthful king of some 3,200 years ago in all its beauty and frailty. It was unique because most tombs had been ransacked thousands of years before, and what was left had been poorly conserved and often destroyed by excavators. Carter, who always put conservation first, made sure that this time the "wonderful things" were not pillaged by the 20th-century world.

Tutankhamun's gilded statue mounted on the back of a black leopard reflects the Egyptian belief that after death the king passed through the dark underworld.

4

The Last "Lost" Tomb?

oward the end of the 20th century, most archaeologists were sure there was nothing new to be found in Valley of the Kings. But in 1973 Kent Weeks, at that time director of the renowned Chicago House, the University of Chicago's Oriental Institute headquarters in Luxor, realized that an up-to-date, comprehensive map of Valley of the Kings was urgently needed. A map would not only document the Valley but also assess the tombs to help stop their continuing deterioration. In 1979 he was able to raise enough money to establish what became the Theban Mapping Project (TMP). Gone were the days of wealthy patrons like Theodore Davis and the Earl of Carnarvon.

Professional surveyor David Goodman uses a theodolite (an instrument used to measure vertical and horizontal angles) to map the cliffs above Deir el-Bahari. Even with such modern expertise, it took 10 years to map Valley of the Kings.

Weeks, today a professor of Egyptology at the American University at Cairo, had assumed that making architectural plans of the tombs in the Valley would be "simple and straightforward." To his surprise, even with a talented team of surveyors, engineers, and students of archaeology using technologically advanced equipment, the job he thought could be accomplished in a few days took 10 years.

Even after its completion, Weeks wanted to devote one last season to finding 13 tombs that had "gone missing." These were tombs that had been mentioned in 18th- or 19th-century documents but the locations of which were no longer known. The best way to search was for the TMP team to carry a magnetometer (which looks like a shoebox taped to a walking stick), as they walked along the hillsides. Although the magnetometer cannot locate a tomb, by measuring the intensity of magnetic fields it shows where there are differences beneath the surface—unusual spaces or walls that might indicate a tomb.

A young Stuart Tyson Smith uses a theodolite with an infrared distance measurer (an early version of the Total Station) to map Valley of the Kings. Smith did his first field work with the Theban Mapping Project.

Professor Weeks was particularly eager to relocate KV 5, which, according to 19th-century maps, was located near the Valley's entrance. In 1825 James Burton had explored it briefly, and his sketched maps would prove of great value. Furthermore, there was the immediate danger of losing the tomb forever.

The Egyptian Antiquities Organization (formerly the Antiquities Service) intended to widen the roadway so that parking would be available for scores of tourist buses. If the tomb was nearby, the widening would damage it

Mapping with Lasers

One of the most important things that sets archaeologists apart from tomb robbers is that they document their finds, carefully mapping the sites and recording the positions of the artifacts found there. A computerized surveying instrument called a Total Station makes it possible to do this much faster and more accurately than in years past. These high-tech instruments look a lot like a conventional surveyor's transit, an instrument with a telescope used to measure horizontal and vertical angles. But the older surveying instruments only provided measurements of the horizontal and vertical angles to the point being recorded. To really establish its location, the distance is also needed. This used to be measured directly with a tape measure, a special chain, or a stadia rod marked to provide a visual estimation of distance through the telescope. All these methods were inaccurate.

A Total Station measures angles with great precision, and it accurately determines distances using infrared and laser technology. A beam of infrared light (or a laser) goes to the target and bounces back to the Total Station, which records the length of time it took to go back and forth. Because light travels at a constant speed, a built-in computer can calculate the exact distance. Combining the distance with the angles, the computer can establish the exact location of objects such as an ushabti, architecture such as tombs, and geographical features of the Valley itself, in relation to one another. When this information is downloaded to a laptop or desktop computer, special programs can make a detailed and highly accurate map. Kent Weeks's Theban Mapping Project has used this technology (shown on page 30) to make the first truly precise map of Valley of the Kings and all the tombs in it.

permanently, so it was essential to find its exact location. In the summer of 1989 the Egyptian Antiquities Organization agreed to let the search for KV 5 begin.

Weeks and his team began looking for the channel where Burton had entered the tomb. Within a week they exposed a badly worn staircase cut into the bedrock that led to a doorway. Debris covered the doorway and the chamber beyond, but James Burton's 1825 channel was still there after 164 years.

Workmen removed several large stones so that Weeks and his assistant archaeologist Catharine Roehrig could climb down into the pit. As they did, foul air rushed up at them from a tourist cafeteria's broken sewer line that had been flowing into the site since the 1950s. The place smelled terrible and had to be cleaned before work could progress.

In the meantime, Roehrig and Weeks examined the exposed part of the doorjambs and could see a faint cartouche—that of Ramesses II. Days later, as the channel became more accessible, Weeks, Roehrig, and their chief workman, Mohammed, could see decoration on every wall. They had located KV 5, and it was not just "an unimportant, undecorated, unused hole" as the early explorers had thought.

The next season proved that it would not be easy to clear KV 5. In fact, the slow and meticulous process of clearing the first three rooms would take four years. Soon it became obvious that the tourist buses that had been stopping only 15 feet from its entrance since 1950 had seriously weakened the walls and pillars that supported the roof. Clearing had to be done carefully.

Floods had filled Chamber One to the ceiling and made the debris almost as hard as concrete. Only two men at a time,

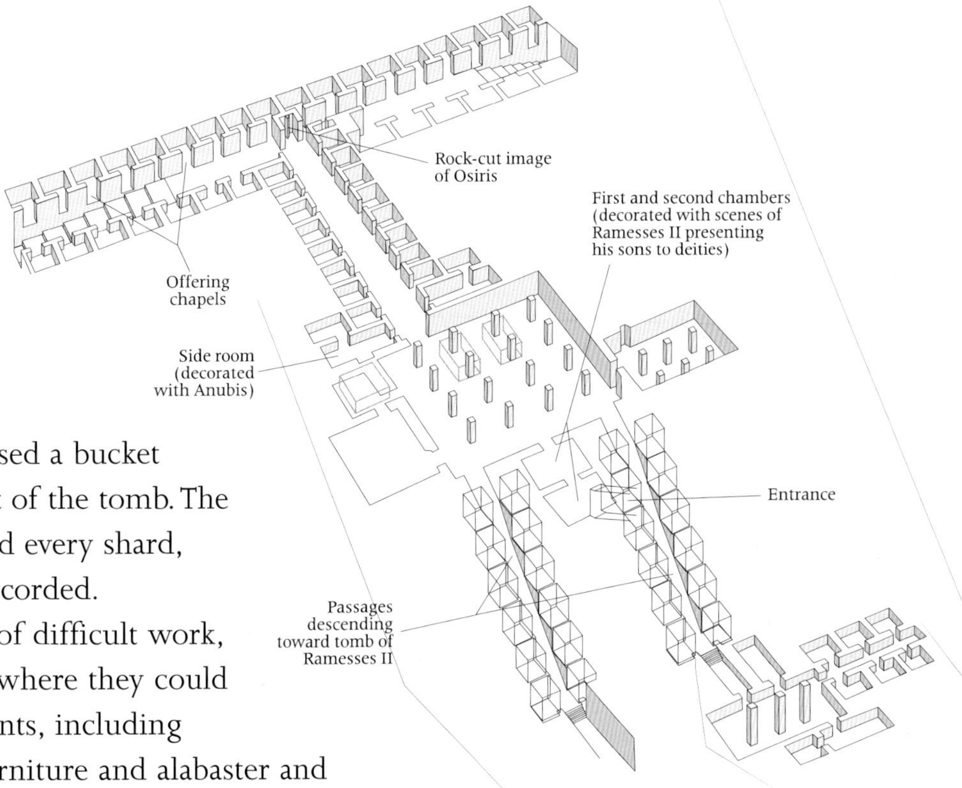

Rock-cut image
of Osiris

First and second chambers
(decorated with scenes of
Ramesses II presenting
his sons to deities)

Offering
chapels

Side room
(decorated
with Anubis)

Entrance

Passages
descending
toward tomb of
Ramesses II

Mohammed and his assistant, Hussein, could pick-ax the dense material and break it up for the 10 men behind them, who used a bucket brigade to take it out of the tomb. The rubble was sifted, and every shard, bone, or bead was recorded.

After two weeks of difficult work, they reached a level where they could see countless fragments, including pieces of wooden furniture and alabaster and faience (glazed ceramic) ushabtis. After a month, Weeks carefully pulled away the uppermost part of the debris from the wall and found traces of hieroglyphs that said: *Sa nesu tepy*—"The Eldest Son of the King."

Over the next seasons, the tedious work continued, and another scene and inscription were uncovered that showed the figure of the king's second son, another Ramesses. Now KV 5 was more than just a lost tomb. As Weeks says, "The burial place of sons of so powerful and important a pharaoh was of potentially great historical importance." Maybe, thought Weeks, in another season or two the team could survey, clear, conserve, and stabilize the chambers as well as study its objects and decorations. He was far too optimistic. By 2001, it had taken 12 years and much yet remained to be done.

In the 1995 season, as the team cleared the first three chambers, they realized that a long corridor went deep into the hillside.

This diagram shows some of the 150 rooms that Kent Weeks's excavation of KV 5 has revealed so far. The future may bring even more surprises.

Osiris was originally a grain god whose life, death, and rebirth followed the agricultural cycle, making him a potent symbol of rejuvenation in the afterlife. His image appears frequently on tomb decorations in the Valley, as here in KV 5.

Removing the debris, Weeks and a young Egyptologist named Marjorie Aronow made their way through the rubble and saw that the corridor was about six feet wide. In the light of their flashlights they could see that the walls had many doorways, which was very unusual. As they went further, the beams of light fell on a five-foot-tall statue located in a niche. It was a beautiful standing figure of Osiris, ancient Egypt's most important god of the afterlife.

Doorways flanked the statue. Surprisingly, they did not lead into side chambers, but into more corridors that went deeper into the bedrock with still more doorways cut into their walls. Counting the doorways, Weeks and Aronow were speechless. They figured out that there must be more than 65 chambers. No other tomb discovered in Valley of the Kings—or for that matter in all Egypt—had more than 30 chambers. By 1997, more corridors and more rooms were found. Weeks and his team estimated that there must be at least 150 rooms.

By 2001 only 7 percent of the tomb had been cleared. There is little chance that "treasure" will be found here, as repeated robberies 3,000 years ago had stripped the tomb of metals, oils, and linens. But what is left of artifacts, reliefs, and the architecture itself will enable archaeologists to reconstruct the story of the final resting place of the sons of Ramesses the Great and bring together new knowledge about their era.

5

Where Did All the Mummies Go?

At the end of the New Kingdom, priests in charge of Valley of the Kings could no longer ignore the constant violation of tombs and their mummified sacred kings. So about 1000 BC, and probably for the next 100 years, officials and priests moved the mummies not once but many times out of the necropolis (ancient burial area). Unceremoniously transferred, the mummies lost most of their original burial ornaments and other trappings along the way. Ironically, robbers had been rifling and destroying the tombs for years, but when the mummies were restored and rewrapped, probably in Dynasty 22, the final stripping

An enormous cache of royal and royal family mummies was found in the cliffs of Deir el-Bahari, near the elegant temple of Queen Hatshepsut

was done by the authorities themselves, hungry for gold at a time when Egypt was in serious decline. One of their final resting places was in a hidden tomb in the cliffs of Deir el-Bahari.

In the 1870s and 1880s, a notorious Egyptian family of robbers were "mining" a cache of very fine artifacts. Careful not to arouse the suspicion that a horde of royal objects on the antiquities market would cause, they brought out a few treasures at a time. Finally, one disgruntled family member led Emile Brugsch, assistant to Gaston Maspero, to the cache in the cliffs. When Brugsch was lowered into the tomb on a hot summer day in 1881, he found the mummies of more than 50 kings, queens, lesser royalty, and courtiers along with some 6,000 objects. Other than the robber family, no one had been in the hidden tomb for 3,000 years. The find was staggering.

Before 1881, kings had been just names attached to statues, reliefs, and papyrus. Now, archaeologists could gaze at the mummified faces of some of the greatest kings of antiquity, among them Ahmose I (first king of the New Kingdom), Tuthmosis III, Seti I,

The scar across this Theban mummy's abdomen indicates that he received the "deluxe" treatment. Such advanced mummification included the removal and separate embalming of the internal organs—except the heart, which ancient Egyptians considered the seat of the soul.

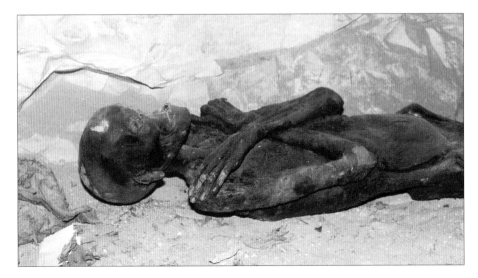

and Ramesses II. Within days, the tomb was emptied and the extraordinary cache was transferred to the museum in Cairo. But the rapid clearance by museum authorities was an archaeological disaster. The discovery was published with illustrations and photos, but without mention of precise locations where the mummies and objects had been found.

Maspero organized an unwrapping event watched over by important officials. The haphazard affair began by discarding the mummy wrappings with writing on them. Finally, the exposed body of Tuthmosis III, called the Napoléon of his time, was revealed with his legs broken off at the pelvic joints, head snapped from the neck. Maspero was so disheartened that he did not unwrap another king for several years.

In 1898 another stunning cache was found in the tomb of Amenhotep II (KV 35). Within the chamber were bodies in coffins with cartouches still readable; among the royal mummies were Tuthmosis IV, Amenhotep III, Merneptah, and Ramesses IV, V, and VI. Amenhotep II lay in his stone sarcophagus, the only New Kingdom pharaoh other than Tutankhamun to remain in his own tomb. Modern studies have shown that these mummies had also been collected from various tombs and earlier caches and hidden away in ancient times.

The archaeological methods of the late 20th and early 21st centuries are a sharp contrast to most earlier excavations. Beginning in 1998, the Amarna Royal Tombs Project directed by Nicholas Reeves and Geoffrey Martin, recleared the "Gold Tomb" that Davis had excavated in 1908. Besides finding gold leaf and a small gold necklace that Davis missed, they produced a computerized three-dimensional plan. Now the team has begun excavating below what was

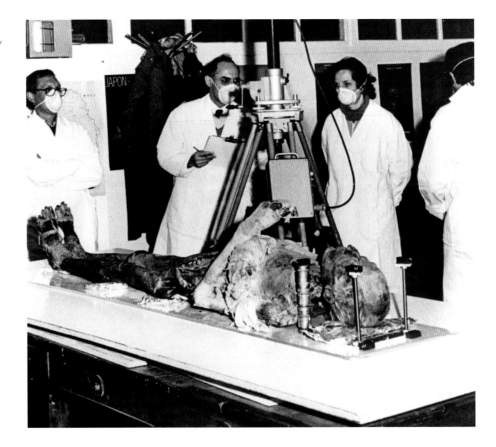

In 1975 an honor guard met Ramesses II's mummy upon its arrival in Paris for conservation work. Ramesses lived to be 90, and when these scientists X rayed his mummy it showed the typical ailments of old age.

once considered bedrock in hope of finding more undiscovered tombs on the same level where Tutankhamun's tomb was found.

Computers are an integral part of the new methods. For instance, measuring tapes have been replaced by computerized theodolites (surveying instruments) that allow archaeologists to map sites and place objects accurately by measuring distances with infrared and laser technology.

Research on mummies has included a comprehensive X-ray study of royal mummies by Egyptologist James Harris's team. Also, mass spectrometry on 13 mummies in the British Museum showed researcher Stephen Buckley that Egyptian embalmers used plant oils that acted as antibiotics, killing microbes to help preserve the bodies.

Mummies are being DNA-tested to show the relationships between individuals, which is particularly helpful in understanding who is related to whom in the families of Dynasty 18. For example, Akhenaten may have been Tutankhamun's father. However, Akhenaten, as seen in statues, with long, exaggerated facial features and slightly feminine physique, looks markedly different from Tutankhamun's portraits and those of other possible relations.

Some scholars suspect his bizarre portraits to be an indication of disease. Others propose that it is an art style. Archaeologists tested these two hypotheses by checking the mummies of Tutankhamun's stillborn infants for signs of genetic disease. No genetic problems were found, which supports the scholars who propose that Akhenaten's strange appearance is an art style.

To deal with the frequent flooding of the tombs, geologists, engineers, and hydrologists are engaged in other aspects of preservation working alongside archaeologists. With modern methods and conservation techniques, there is still a great deal to learn from Valley of the Kings.

Pharaoh Akhenaten's portraits show him with feminine features such as a slender waist and round hips. Some experts think these traits were due to disease but others suggest they were the art style of his era.

Interview with Stuart Tyson Smith

Nancy Stone Bernard How did you get interested in archaeology?

Stuart Tyson Smith When I was in fifth grade, I lived in Palos Verdes, California, and I participated in an enrichment program taught by an amateur archaeologist. I especially loved the story of how Howard Carter, in discovering King Tut's tomb, stepped back in time some 3,200 years. The immediacy of the past appealed to me. The story of Carter finding a bundle of rings near the entrance of the tomb made me imagine all kinds of possibilities. Did the robbers drop the bundle as they were running out of the tomb? Did they lose it when their oil lamps were too dim to see where they dropped it? Or did the "police" arrive and, in the robbers' haste, they dropped it? My interest continued in high school. I read all the Egypt books I could find.

NSB When you began college, did you know the direction you would go?

STS Not really. I went to the University of California at Berkeley and became an anthropology major. I knew I wanted to be an archaeologist, but not necessarily an Egyptologist. Then I was inspired by Professor Kent Weeks. He took me to Egypt

(top) Stuart Tyson Smith joins some of the cast of Stargate on the movie's set.
(bottom) Nancy Stone Bernard visits Stuart Tyson Smith at his office at the University of California, Santa Barbara.

as a student and I worked on the Theban Mapping Project with him. I spent about three months in Luxor working in the field.

NSB What were some of your most interesting digs?

STS Egypt and Nubia, now the Sudan, have been the most exciting. The project I'm now investigating, located near the third cataract in Nubia, is called the Dongola Reach Expedition. We're concentrating on ancient Egyptian tombs of late Dynasty 18. We've discovered the remains of a pyramid as well as tombs that range from 1450 to 1100 BC We're trying to find out how long these ancient Egyptian colonists stayed and how they influenced the Nubian population that surrounded them in great numbers.

NSB Have you had any especially exciting experiences?

STS With the Theban Mapping Project, we rappelled off the cliffs as an exciting way to investigate possible cave burial sites. But the most extraordinary adventure was one hot air balloon ride. Normally (and you can do this as a tourist), you shoot up to about 2,300 feet and then hover over the Theban necropolis. We did that and had a gorgeous view of the valleys, but instead of going where we were supposed to, we were taken farther and farther west by the wind, out to the Sahara Desert. We had to land. The pilot started descending, down and down, right next to the tiered cliffs,

but just as we would get close, the wind would take us up again. Finally, the pilot said, "Hold on, we're going to have to crash land." Fortunately we crashed near some quarries where there was a road. Our chase car was able to rescue us. No one was hurt, but it was exciting.

NSB We understand that you have served as a consultant to the movies. Which movies were they?

STS *Stargate*, *The Mummy*, and *The Mummy Returns*.

NSB What kind of advice did you give, and did they take it?

STS First, the producers of *Stargate* asked me if I could work on creating catchy graphics with hieroglyphs fading into English at the beginning of the film. Of course, the plot was silly. Space aliens did not build the pyramids, but the story called for an archaeologist who goes to the planet where the supposed builders came from. He had to speak ancient Egyptian, and the producers asked me if I could figure out how it would sound.

Hieroglyphs look like picture writing but they actually have phonetic meaning; the only trouble is the words don't have vowels. I figured out a spoken language based on ancient Egyptian hieroglyphs. This was a first in the movies. The actors who spoke the language did a great job. This dialogue was actually ancient Egyptian from about the time of King Tut. I was invited on the set, which was near the sand dunes of Yuma, Arizona. I worked with actor James Spader, who took the part of the archaeologist. I coached him, and it's been said that he is the most believable archaeologist ever played in the movies. In fact, not surprisingly, my friends say Spader's character reminds them of me.

NSB How did you get the jobs on the *Mummy* pictures?

STS One of the actors who had been in *Stargate* knew about my work. The producers asked me to comment on the script, which I did. For instance, I pointed out that there are only four canopic jars in a tomb, not five, but they didn't take that advice. However, when I said you can't have these people using iron and steel—they weren't invented yet—they did listen. And when they wanted to have a treasure room full of gemstones, I told them the Egyptians didn't have gemstones. They did adjust that.

I was asked again for *The Mummy Returns*. I made language tapes for the actors, and the female villain ended up with especially excellent pronunciation. Overall, the dialog in *The Mummy Returns* came out really well. I'm happy the producers wanted to lend some authenticity to their movie because it sparks the audience's interest to find out the real story of ancient Egypt.

NSB What is your advice to a young person who wants to make archaeology a career?

STS The first thing is, you have to love it. You have to be dedicated and focused. It's not an easy profession. There are not a lot of jobs, and the job market is very competitive. You don't make a lot of money. Although, you can be an amateur and continue your interest by being involved with local archaeological societies. But mostly you have to be a good puzzle-solver. It's like putting together jigsaw puzzles, but we have only half the pieces. Another neat thing is that anyone who works in a different part of the world shares new experiences and insights into foreign cultures.

Lastly, you have to like to write. It's not just digging. You take notes in the field and you have to figure out what you are finding and publish the story. I enjoy the writing and drawing conclusions because, to quote the famous archaeologist Flinders Petrie, "Archaeology brings people back to life." Currently, I'm digging in a forgotten cemetery for people who have been "lost" for thousands of years. When we found a beautiful Mycenaean pilgrim flask in a Nubian cemetery, we were bringing people back, trying to figure why an artifact from the ancient Greek world showed up in the desert south of Egypt. For me, to make some sense of this puzzle—that's what's cool.

Glossary

Amarna art Stylized, naturalistic art that appears just before and during Pharaoh Akhenaten's reign. Different from the formal, rather stiff figures of previous eras. Named for Akhenaten's capital at Tel el-Amarna.

Amarna letters Important cache of Dynasty 18 cuneiform tablets discovered at Tel el-Amarna in 1887.

Amun Most powerful god of the New Kingdom. During the New Kingdom he was linked to the sun god Re, thus becoming Amun-Re.

antiquities Artifacts from ancient times.

Anubis Jackal-headed god of the dead, closely associated with embalming and mummification.

bitumen Substance similar to asphalt or pitch, used as cement. The darkened resins used in mummification were mistaken for bitumen, or *mummia* in Arabic, from which the word mummy is derived.

canopic jars Stone and ceramic vessels used to store internal organs that were removed during the mummification process.

cartouche An oval-shaped loop that represented eternity as a never-ending knotted rope; within the loop, a royal name was inscribed in hieroglyphs.

cuneiform Type of writing incised on clay tablets with the triangular-shaped end of a stylus. Developed in Mesopotamia. The name is derived from the Latin word for "wedge-shaped."

dynasty A related ruling family.

hieroglyphs Egyptian script, based on sounds, arranged in continuous horizontal and vertical lines without any punctuation or spaces. It is usually read from right to left and top to bottom. In use from about 3200 BC to the 4th century AD

mummy A preserved corpse.

mummification The process by which corpses were preserved by taking out the organs, then placing natron, a salt, over and around the body. After 40 days, during which 75 percent of body weight was lost, the body was packed with fresh natron bags to give it a natural shape. The whole body was coated with resin, darkening the color of the skin, and then bandaged with strips of linen. After 70 days the process was complete.

Near East The territory northeast of Egypt that several Egyptian kings conquered during different periods. People from the area were called Asiatics by the ancient Egyptians.

necropolis Large and important burial areas that were used in all Egyptian periods. The term is from the Greek meaning "city of the dead."

New Kingdom One of the periods of ancient Egypt, lasting from 1550 BC to about 1070 BC.

obelisk Large tapering stone shaft with a pyramid-shaped top. Considered a sun symbol, obelisks were often set up in pairs outside entrances to important temples.

Osiris One of the earliest and most important ancient Egyptian gods, associated with death, resurrection, and fertility. He is usually depicted as a mummy whose hands project through his wrappings to hold the royal insignias of crook (a farmer's staff) and flail (a threshing tool).

papyrus Principal Egyptian writing material. It is a reed that grew profusely in the Delta region of Lower Egypt. When split into strips that were laid side-by-side and dried, it became a strong material on which to write.

pharaoh Beginning in the New Kingdom, the title used for the king of Egypt. The word is derived from the word for the royal palace, the *per-aa*, or "great house."

Rosetta Stone Black granite stela found in 1799 by a French army officer at the village of el-Rashid (Rosetta) in the Delta region of Egypt. Originally erected in 196 BC, it was inscribed with three writings: hieroglyphs, demotic (popular, cursive Egyptian script), and Greek.

sarcophagus (plural, **sarcophagi**) Outer container of a coffin, usually made of stone. In Egypt, it was often decorated with magic spells in hieroglyphs.

Sea Peoples Wandering folk of the 12th century BC who attacked many places in the Mediterranean world. They are especially known from reliefs at Medinet Habu and Karnak in the reign of Ramesses III.

shard Fragment of broken pottery.

stela (plural, **stelae**) Upright slab of stone or wood inscribed with texts or sculpted reliefs.

ushabti Small statue of a mummy placed in a tomb to work on behalf of the deceased in the afterlife.

Further Reading

Baines, John, and Jaromir Malek. *Cultural Atlas of Ancient Egypt*. New York: Facts on File, 2000.

Baker, Charles, and Rosalie Baker. *Ancient Egyptians: People of the Pyramids*. New York: Oxford University Press, 2001.

Brier, Bob. *The Encyclopedia of Mummies*. New York: Facts on File, 1998.

Carter, Howard. *The Tomb of Tut.ankh.Amen: The Burial Chamber*. 1923. Reprint, London: Duckworth, 2000.

Carter, Howard. *The Tomb of Tut.ankh.Amen, Discovered by the Late Earl of Carnarvon and Howard Carter: The Annex and Treasury*. 1923. Reprint, London: Duckworth, 2000.

Carter, Howard, and A. C. Mace. *The Discovery of the Tomb of Tutankamen*. 1923. Reprint, Mineola, N.Y.: Dover, 1977.

Clayton, Peter A. *Chronicle of the Pharaohs: The Reign-by-Reign Record of the Rulers and Dynasties of Ancient Egypt*. New York: Thames & Hudson, 1994.

Donoghue, Carol. *The Mystery of the Hieroglyphs*. New York: Oxford University Press, 1999.

Green, Robert. *Tutankhamun*. New York: Watts, 1996.

Perl, Lila. *Mummies, Tombs, and Treasure*. New York: Clarion, 1987.

Reeves, C. Nicholas. *Ancient Egypt: The Great Discoveries: A Year-by-Year Chronicle*. New York: Thames & Hudson, 2000.

Reeves, C. Nicholas, and Richard H. Wilkinson. *The Complete Valley of the Kings: Tombs and Treasures of Egypt's Greatest Pharaohs*. New York: Thames & Hudson, 1996.

Reeves, C. Nicholas. *The Complete Tutankhamun: The King, the Tomb, the Royal Treasure*. New York: Thames & Hudson, 1990.

Romer, John. *Ancient Lives: Daily Life in Egypt of the Pharaohs*. New York: Harcourt Brace, 1984.

Romer, John. *Valley of the Kings: Exploring the Tombs of the Pharaohs*. New York: William Morrow, 1994.

Shaw, Ian, and Paul Nicholson. *Dictionary of Ancient Egypt*. New York: Abrams, 1995.

Weeks, Kent R. *The Lost Tomb*. New York: William Morrow, 1998.

Related Sites

COLOSSI OF MEMNON

West bank of the Nile, across from Luxor (ancient Thebes)

These two huge 65-foot quartzite figures sitting on gigantic thrones are portraits of Amenhotep III that decorated the front of his now-vanished mortuary temple. An earthquake in 27 BC caused a crack in the northern statue. As it was warmed by the early morning rays of the sun, it would produce an eerie moan. More than 150 years later, a Roman emperor restored the statue, silencing the noise forever.

DEIR EL-BAHARI

West bank of the Nile, just east of Valley of the Kings

One of the most beautiful remaining buildings of ancient Egypt, the temple of Queen Hatshepsut, lies nestled against a bay in the cliffs. The limestone temple rises in three terraces. Within the temple are reliefs and painted walls with scenes from her reign. Just to the south are the few remains of the temple of King Mentuhotep of the Middle Kingdom, some 500 years earlier.

MEDINET HABU

West bank, across the Nile from southern Luxor

This huge mortuary temple of Ramesses III, the pharaoh who fought the Sea Peoples in 1189 BC, is the best example of the layout of a New Kingdom temple. Its enormous outer courtyards are known for their colorful inscribed walls.

RAMESSEUM

West bank, across the Nile from Luxor

The mortuary temple of Ramesses II is known for the huge fallen granite statue of the pharaoh, which inspired the 19th-century English poet Percy Bysshe Shelley to write *Ozymandias* about the futility of a tyrant's power.

TEMPLE OF KARNAK

In the town of Luxor

The approach to this enormous 200-acre temple is through an avenue of sphinxes that once linked the temples of Karnak and Luxor. The immense Hypostyle Hall has 134 inscribed columns. Dedicated to the god Amun, it was begun by Amenhotep III and finished by Seti I and Ramesses II. Many other kings added to the temple. Ramesses II inscribed the story of the important Egyptian-Hittite battle of Kadesh and the peace treaty that followed.

TEMPLE OF LUXOR

In the center of Luxor, not far from Karnak

The Luxor temple was mainly the work of Amenhotep III and Ramesses II. Many other kings left their mark, including Tutankhamun. There are even rooms here from Roman times.

THE WORKMEN'S VILLAGE

Deir el-Medina lies on the path between Deir el-Bahari and Valley of the Queens

The walled village is the site of a number of ancient houses and well-preserved, colorfully painted underground tombs of workmen who were employed in the nearby necropolis of Valley of the Kings.

Crafted more than 4,000 years ago, this model depicts life at a country village like Deir el-Medina.

Index

Stuart Tyson Smith is an associate professor of anthropology at the University of California, Santa Barbara. He has worked on five archaeological projects in Egypt, including three in the Theban Necropolis (the first with Kent Weeks's Theban Mapping Project). He currently directs the University of California Dongola Reach Expedition in northern Sudan, exploring the impact of Egyptian colonialism on Nubia during the time of Valley of the Kings. In 1993, he took a break from academics to work as an Egyptology consultant to the science fiction movie *Stargate*. He has since worked on *The Mummy* and *The Mummy Returns*.

Nancy Stone Bernard has written several books on archaeology for young people. She founded and is the director of the Archaeological Associates of Greenwich, Connecticut, a non-profit organization dedicated to educating the general public about archaeology. She served for six years on the governing board of the Archaeological Institute of America as its education chair. She has taught continuing education classes in archaeology and an enrichment program in prehistory to pre-collegiate students, first in Los Angeles, California, and for many years in Greenwich, Connecticut. She is currently on the editorial advisory board of *DIG* magazine.

Brian Fagan is Professor of Anthropology at the University of California, Santa Barbara. He is internationally known for his books on archaeology, among them *The Adventure of Archaeology*, *The Rape of the Nile*, and *The Oxford Companion to Archaeology*.

digging
for the past

Sites in This Series

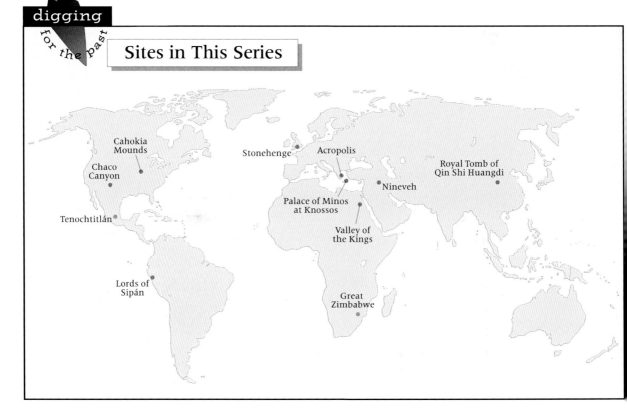

Cahokia Mounds
Chaco Canyon
Stonehenge
Acropolis
Royal Tomb of Qin Shi Huangdi
Nineveh
Palace of Minos at Knossos
Tenochtitlán
Valley of the Kings
Lords of Sipán
Great Zimbabwe